PLEASURE TO SOUL

POETRIES FROM MY HEART TO YOUR SOUL.

NEHA BISHT

To the people,

who ever felt *left out* or *different*.

Contents

Foreword

When I read the content of this book, and the work done. I just imagined my teenage days, when I also faced the societal pressure and peer issues. but this book is not about peer issues but this about the time we have now, the carelessness and the occurence in lives of the people living around.

I never saw this wide view about nowadays generations, and one ever wrote this openely about today's incidents.

Some of them really got me out of my mind. The love and affection, that is put in the work shows the ambition of becoming a well known poet.

Being a flowering Author, this work is appreciatable.

Preface

A small introduction of this work, I don't think will be able to explain what's inside the book. But for the context of preface, the reason of me writing this book is write below.

I was there in my teenage, when everyone used to compare me to the people, I didn't even had any connection with. I had many friends but suddenly I lost connection with everyone around, and felt that I find peace when I am alone. Then, I started writing things I felt I could share with people close to me. Each and every poem inside this book is the evidence of me being alone. But the issue I faced was preserving my work, then I got a suggestion from rarely existing people in my life to compile them as a book and let the world read what I have written.

This book and every piece inside it, these are not just words for me but they are a phase of my life. I never thought I would compile it into a book, and let everyone read it. But yes I'm doing it for people like me.

After all, we never know what happens next,

So, let's save every phase in the form of text.

1. Fire to Ice

You don't wanna talk, ok just dont.
You don't wanna be in touch, ok just don't.
But remember!
Once this phase starts it has no end
You don't care, ok just don't.
You think I'm not fair, ok just don't.
I hope you know, I have got a bad anger.
Once you got my mind, baby you gonna get a trigger.
It's better for you to be away,
Coz it's hard for you to stand n stay.
Just let me burn in my own issues,
And turn into a girl living in Igloos.
Coldness of my mind is good for everyone,
Or else the whole world is under my impression.

2. Darkness

The sparks in my life were fading,
The darkness grew wide.
This was me draining,
And the silence was bonafide.
As the time passed, Darkness embraced me.
I hated the light that betrayed me.
Tho you don't know what is right,
But my dear you know this night.
A sunshine is waiting for you besides,
Hold your hopes just hold them tight.
You know why?
Coz it's a Good Night!

3. Shopping with Mom

I loved shopping until I went to a mall
My mother was my company and no one else at all.
I thought she would love the new fashion
But no, criticising it was her passion.
She had a creepy look whenever saw girl's wear
And starting chanting- wearing these was a dare.
I knew she won't let me buy these things,
So, I made her to be at 'Christmas Brings.'
Collected the new arrival from the shop,
But unfortunately I didn't had a job.
My mother wasn't paying for the things I brought,
And I knew my wardrobe is going to face a drought.
Returned with a face extremely down,
And took a pledge-

'I don't know whatever happens

But shopping with Mom

Is not even my mind's around.'

4. Thoughts I Encounter

Your existence till eternity.
My faith is eternal.
Oo my Dear God
Guide me, to be humble.
Whatever is the situation I'll deal with it surely,
This kind of confidence is seen very rarely.
I totally understand the concept you have made,
Confidential is the life that is under the shade.
The realistic thought I have ever Encountered,
Footsteps of Death are always unheard.
I'm there in the progress of clearing my mind,
Uniting my soul with the soul undefined.
Somewhere in this process I'll find peace.
And there my God!
Will be the end of your Masterpiece.

5. Goodbye

I want to run, I want to hide
From all the pain, he caused inside
I want to scream, I want to cry
Why can't I tell him Goodbye?
I want to move on; I just can't let it go
I love him more than he'll ever know
I want to start over; I want to feel free!
But this pain will never let me be.
He hurt me bad, the pain is deep
From all the promises he couldn't keep
All the lies I heard him say
Are there in my head and just won't fade
The love I gave him, that I never got back
The support I provided wasn't a piece of cake
I don't know if he ever loved me
Or I was the only one, thinking he's into me.

6. Love is Blind

He is wildfire to my field

And flood to my lowlands

I burn to his touch yet, I drown when he's distant.

He is beautiful as Adonis

And deadly as Echidna

I could die in his arms, but I think he'll kill me sooner.

As if his heart looked at Medusa, and now it's all stone.

He slowly pushes the knife into me

Smiling calmly, how peaceful.

He cuddles on cold nights,

And shoulders when the soul cries,

I want to always be with him but he's the reason for my wet eyes.

He is bright as sun,

And gentle as drizzling rain,

Enchanting an ancient lore,

He'll trade my soul for nothing.

I threw him away and like a Boomerang, he came back.

I pushed him away and like a wind carrying dead leaves, he floated back.

I buried him underground and like an undead, he rose back.

I succumbed to the esctasy,

My addiction to the sweet prison got the better of me.

I'm with him,

It hurts but it also alliviates.

His heart looked at Medusa and now it's all stone.

Now I know what they mean when they say,
'Love is blind, Darling!'
You can't see red flags if you don't open your eyes, Darling.

7. Awake till morning

Lately I find myself
Awake till the morning.
Coz if I don't sleep in the night then
The nightmare might come to a stop, right?
Coz every dream feels like Deja-vu
I get to live in pain, twice.
Every decision feels like a sharp knife
On which my life has to fall, right?
And stab everything,
There is blood everywhere,
Only my eyes are able to spot them.
I clean it with the lies I tell to myself.
'It's all my fault?' 'It's not my fault.'
'It's not my fault.' 'It's all my fault?'
In a loop these words repeat in my head,
I fight with myself and then loose to myself.
Sometimes I scream- when I'm alone,
Sometimes I whisper- when somebody's home.
But not to be saved, just to say them out loud,
Coz you can't save me,
And that's not once fault.
I don't sleep well.
I don't wake up right.
There is nothing wrong here, and then everything is.

I never knew love,

Coz I never loved enough.

And everytime I laugh, I suffocate.

Now lately I find myself, awake till the morning.

Coz if I don't sleep in the night then

The nightmare might come to a stop, right?

8. A Night Full Of Stars

Darkness everywhere
I desired the light to be nowhere.
Coz,
Baby, stars were glowing and I had eyes on them.
I knew I couldn't save our life problem.
Those glittering spots were attracting me,
I blushed imagining you with glee.
Thinking of you, holding my hand,
The warmness of you, that I couldn't stand.
Telling you honestly, I'm not a sky gazer,
But Darling! With you I can't even stand a Breezer.
You know my heart skips a beat,
When I see you that also in repeat.
This night is full of stars and memories of you,
I miss the moments, the moments were few.
Few in count, but are full of love
Baby, you don't know but you are enough.

9. Home Alone

You know being in a home, all alone
Baby feels so bad, when it's your own home.
The little tiny heart is not happy now,
The guilt of being here, is just eating me how?
Letting you down, begging for you
I hitted my least, just for you.
I know you dont know,
The feeling of mine.
Baby I wanna confess,
The feeling of mine.
Ya I'm into you, I mean
Ya I love you.
Ya I'm into you, I mean
Ya I do love you.

10. A Fact of Life

I didn't knew what was happening,
I still thought it was frightening.
Just went for walk,
Realised I had nothing to talk.
Trying to feel the beauty of nature,
Trying to understand all the created creature.
Everyone had their own sorrows,
And some were pointers over the arrows.
I was still silent,
But I felt a less violent.
I understood the fact of life,

That whatever is going on in it; but the happiness is somewhere alive.

A Thanks To You

We together came to the last of this book.

    That was short but a long felt journey,

    I have gratitutde in my heart, for you

    As by reading this book you became a part of my life.

Write To Me

Being a self published author, A review is very essential for my upcoming work.

So, do write to me about iT.

Socials;-

Instagram;- writer.neha

Twitter;- neha0126

Mail; nehabisht0126@gmail.com

Your feedback is precious.

Next

Dear readers,

The work full of love is there in the line, to be published.

It is all about the war going between the head and heart.

Relatable right?

This is not the end,

This is the beginning of your Era, Dear!

www.ingramcontent.com/pod-product-compliance
Lightning Source LLC
Chambersburg PA
CBHW060232170726

48004CB00004BA/1521